Ariel's Song

Published Poems, 1987 - 2023

Dawn Pisturino

Horse Mesa Press

Contents

Acknowledgments

I want to thank my husband and daughter for their steadfast love and support. Without them, this collection would not have been written.

The author owns all rights to previously published poems. They were published under non-exclusive rights (rights revert to the author upon publication.)

"The Listener" and "I HATE SNAKES" appeared originally in *Hidden in Childhood: A Poetry Anthology*, edited by Gabriela Marie Milton and published by Literary Revelations Publishing House.

"Nature's Child" won Honorable Mention in the Arizona Authors Association 2022 Literary Contest and appeared in the *2023 Arizona Literary Magazine*.

"Boudica's Soliloquy" originally appeared in *Wounds I Healed: The Poetry of Strong Women*, edited by Gabriela Marie Milton and published by Ingrid Wilson of Experiments in Fiction Publishing House.

Other poems in this collection were published by Spillwords Press, Literary Revelations Journal, *Underneath the Juniper Tree*, Danse

Macabre du Jour, The Skeptic's Kaddish, Masticadores USA, Gob-
blers & Masticadores, Masticadores India, Chewers & Masticadores,
Hotel Masticadores, Masticadores Magazine (end of the week), Masti-
cadores Barcelona, Horror Sleaze Trash; and in the following antholo-
gies: *Great Poems of Today Anthology* (1987), *World Poetry Antholo-
gy* (1987), *American Poetry Anthology* (1988), *New American Poetry
Anthology* (1988), *Best New Poems of 1988 Anthology,* and *National
Poetry Anthology, 1988.*

Dedication

This book is dedicated to my daughter, Ariel Therese Pisturino.
May music and books surround you wherever you go!

Ashes

A man with a hairy mustache,
Tried to smoke and was turned into ash.
His body was gone, but his ghost lingered on
To sweep himself up for the trash.

First published in the September 2011 issue of *Underneath the Juniper Tree.*

The Man in Galloway Bay

A man lost in Galloway Bay,
    Cried out in a very large bray,
"Please come rescue me, hungry sharks can't agree,
Am I breakfast or dinner entree?"

First published on Underneath the Juniper Tree on July 12, 2011.

The Man from Brazil

T here was an old man from Brazil
    Who ate 'til he made himself ill.
"It's always a treat to eat mangled meat.
I relish the taste of road kill!"

First published on Underneath the Juniper Tree on July 16, 2011.

Published in the August 2011 issue of *Underneath the Juniper Tree.*

The Cannibal and His Dog

A cannibal walking his dog,
Got hungry and sat on a log.
"I'll start with the spleen.
This dog is too lean.
I shouldn't have taught him to jog!"

First published on Underneath the Juniper Tree on July 31, 2011.

Smoking Hot Love

They said smoking would injure my health.
   I lit up a menthol, feeling the cool vapor
Swirl down my throat in a gust of ecstasy.
He found me in the garden, under a tree,
Where the smoke curled around my head,
Like an angel's halo, and caught me in his arms.
Dragging on that butt, I blew smoke rings
Into his mouth. He swallowed them whole.
My coal burned with red-hot passion.
He took it from my fingers and put it to his lips,
Inhaled quietly, and exhaled a gentle
Cloud of smoke across my face.
I breathed it in, inhaling the essence of his love.
He crushed the butt under his foot,
Pulled me to the ground,
And unbuttoned my smoke-perfumed blouse.
My heart burst into flame.

First published on Horror Sleaze Trash on June 21, 2023.

Honey

Honey drips with sweet sensation from her vampire lips,
And the naked round bosom swells with invitation;
Chick is not impressed though his loins beg urgently,
For Death lurks in those baby blue eyes,
And Chick is not prepared to die
For the satisfaction of his loins.
Suddenly the man who bedded a thousand
Is a man with feelings and a sense of pride.
His eyes see new visions in the morning sun.
Life, for him, is more than an elongated erection.
The big word looms in his brain: RELATIONSHIP.
He surveys the choice of women as a connoisseur,
Checking dates and labels, going for the blue ribbon prize.
He awakes alone most mornings now,
But once in a while, in the shadows of night,
A sweet sensation of honey-dew lips caresses his ears,
And Chick is pleasantly surprised:

The woman has a brain.

First published in *The National Poetry Anthology, 1988*.

Nature's Child

S he overflowed with poetry and music and laughter,
    Spilling the boundaries of her life
With delicious rivulets of innocence and joy.
She danced — naked! — in the pure white light of a waxing moon
On a soft, sultry night at the Summer Solstice
And sang to the icicle stars in the middle of winter.
Her nakedness gleamed in moonlight and candlelight,
Sunlight and lamplight,
But she feared not the shadows or the darkness of night.
They called her witch, priestess, sorceress of the Devil.
She laughed at their ignorance —
These holy men of the Church —
And covered her nakedness with rose petals and fern.
Green ivy adorned her wavy red hair —
Long strands of vine cut from ancient oak —
And, in time, she began to resemble the earth itself.
Green moss sprouted between her virgin legs

And beneath her hollow armpits.
Her toenails twisted and curled at the ends of her feet
Like earthbound roots sunk deep into the soil.
Her arms opened wide beneath the golden sun,
Offering prayers and sacrifices to the deity of Life.
She gathered all the richness of sun and rain,
Exulting in the wild green world of her existence.

She withered with the passing years,
As her limbs grew gnarled and bare,
And the birds no longer nested in her hair,
Until hunters from the village
Found her standing on the banks of a gushing stream
And bowed down to worship Nature's Child.

Won Honorable Mention in the Arizona Authors Association 2022 Literary Contest.
First published in the *2023 Arizona Literary Magazine*.

November

When November came,
    We sat around the kitchen table after dark,
Telling chilling tales
Of ghosts and other phantoms of the night,
While wooden logs crackled and burned
On the old stone hearth,
And a cold wind wrapped its spectral arms
Around the ancient wooden cottage.

We warmed ourselves with hot mulled wine
And spiced apple cakes, thickly iced, —
Laughed at our superstitious fears
While trembling in the candlelight.
The old crone, at the stroke of midnight,
Told our fortunes in our hands:
Wedding bells for the shiny-eyed young maid
In spring, and a son born by the end of next year.

The yellow moon peeked in at the windows,
Laughing at our humble ways,
Then rose into the sky on a thousand brooms,
A friendly witness to our midnight celebration.
Holding hands, we danced in the moonlight,
Our cloaks pressed tightly against
The frosty cold; and when morning dawned,
Feathery snowflakes drifted from the sky,
Nature's sign that Winter celebrated, too.

First published on Gobblers & Masticadores on November 4, 2022.

Stars Fade

Time passes, and then we're gone,
   A lump of clay once laughing, laughing no more;
Discarded to the open grave to feed a hungry earth;
A useless, lifeless thing
Long-forgotten in the changing years
But a simple name inscribed on stone;
Unrecognized in the awful pile
Of crumbling clay and moldy dust.
"And where is the sun to warm my aching bones,
And the moon to flame my lover's ardor?
Where is the wind breathing in my ear,
And the life-giving drops of rain?"
Eyes close, and tender hearts stop beating.
So still, so still, the cold black earth (a silent void)
Without the living sounds of hot-blooded life.
Stars fade with life's end;
The coffin lid drops with solemn finality;

And Death remains, cold and intractable,
Yielding not a single ray of light.
Lost to darkness, unseeing, unfeeling wreck
Of human flesh, groping in the dark
For solidness and material comfort!
"I shall not comfort thee;" — and Death hovers over,
Unwanted guardian in our final tribulation.
The soul cries out in black despair: "Lord, take me!"

First published on Danse Macabre du Jour in April 2012.

Published on Masticadores USA on September 22, 2023.

Published on Masticadores Magazine (end of the week) on September 23, 2023.

Published on Masticadores Barcelona on September 23, 2023.

Ariel's Song

A riel sings a lusty song
    Of ships upon the sea,
And ere the night is very long,
Her spell is cast on me.

She spins a web of intrigue,
She tells a tale of woe;
And when the sun is waxing big,
I do not want to go —
No, I do not want to go.

But she folds her wings together
And whispers my release;
For her stories last forever
And her songs will never cease.

Then, she rises from the window,

Winging high into the light,
And I'm left alone in shadow
As she disappears from sight.

First published on Masticadores USA on November 7, 2021.

Rapping

Sometimes, at night,
  I hear the rapping of knuckles on the front door,
Very softly but insistent.
Lying in my bed in fear,
I wonder who could be there,
Rapping on the front door.
I listen intently,
But the dog isn't barking,
And when I pull back the curtains,
No one is there.
The rapping stops, and then I hear it again.
Rap, rap, rap, on the windowpane.
I try to figure out what else
Could rap on the windowpane besides a human being?
My father was not a harmless man when alive,
But he's harmless now, after death,
Except the rap-rap-rapping after dark

On the front door and the windowpane.

And sometimes, the wall. And then it stops.

But once, when I was sitting in a chair,

Reading a book,

The rapping started on the floor,

And I listened to it cross the floor and up the wall

And out the window.

And then I saw him, a black shadow against the wall,

The profile of my father.

I could not believe my eyes and wept,

And told him I loved him.

I asked him not to worry or bear any guilt.

"You must move on," I said, "to a better life."

And then I prayed and burned candles for him

And asked God to take care of him on the Other Side.

But still, after dark, I sometimes hear the rapping

And wonder who or what it could be:

But no one's ever there.

First published on Masticadores USA on August 18, 2022.

Murder House

This house was her prison,
And when she died,
She thought she would be free.

But her soul became trapped
Between the bitter walls —
This house of misery
And pain
And drunkenness
And decay.

This house was her prison,
And when she died,
She thought she would be free.

She was trapped between the walls —
And could not escape —

This house of despair
And loud voices
And violence
And blood.

This house was her prison,
And when she died,
She thought she would be free.

But she remained trapped
Between the walls of her lethal prison —
This house of death
That took her life
And hid her body
Between the walls.

She could not break free.

First published on Masticadores India on March 1, 2023.

Drunken Poet

I'm a drunken poet,
   Whirling around
In the ecstasy of Divine Love.
My heart pounds wildly in my chest,
Beating a staccato drum roll.
My head explodes with divine revelations,
Driving the stars from the heavens.
The sun dances in the sky,
Revolving with bright colors
That blind me.
My ears ring joyously,
My mouth blasts a trumpet's call
That shakes the earth
With a loud rumble.
Oh, divine messengers from God,
Help me grow with the fulness
Of your spirit!

Deliver me from my wicked desires

And bodily complaints.

I want to whirl,

Like a drunken lover,

In the compass of your love.

Let me soar like a dove

On wings of peace

And throw down the weapons of war.

Let me drink the wine of Divine Ecstasy,

Spilling out the sacred words

From my lips.

Lover and beloved.

United. Together.

One Spirit.

One.

First published on Spillwords Press on May 20, 2023.

Evening at the Mosque

I dressed in fine silk
    To meet you in the garden
After evening prayer.
My smile burst through my gauzy veils,
My eyes burned as brightly as the stars
Kissing the minaret,
My happiness flooded the mosque
With the holiest of incense when we met in the crowd.
Our eyes united in mutual longing,
Our hands entwined in love's embrace
As we stole away to the palm-sheltered garden
Laid out in exquisite mosaic
Behind the moonlit house of Allah.
Old women watched us from the shadows,

Monitoring our every move,

Remembering their own fragile youth

And the promise of love's passion,

Lost so many years ago, if ever found at all,

Their husbands, fat old men with white heads,

Muttering in their beards.

We sipped the precious nectar of youth

Flowing from the splashing fountain.

My silken robes fluttered with the desert breeze

That rustled the curious palms

And carried the sweet scent of orange blossoms

Into our eager arms.

The night belonged to us!

Oh, Divine Love, we cried,

Fill us with your invigorating wine

And let us leave this night behind

As drunken lovers.

First published on Masticadores USA on May 21, 2023.

The Last God

When they finally killed their last god,
    The people cried a raucous cheer
And threw their weapons in the air.
Bonfires roared on the tops of hills,
Shimmering in the moonlight.
Chanting and yelling, people danced
'Round the fiery blaze,
Loosened the cords on their loincloths,
And coupled in the evening grass.
Wild and free, they danced until dawn,
Sweating the perfume of naked delight.
And when the sun rose,
Illuminating the start of a new day,
The people cried:
"God is dead!
Humankind has been set free!"

First published on Masticadores USA on June 21, 2023.

Melissa and the Angels

M elissa, in a tattered dress,
     Came slowly down the lane,
A wicker basket on her arm,
Fresh eggs and butter from the farm,
Her tresses in a tangled mess,
Barefoot, and limping with the pain.

Her blue eyes shone with happiness,
For bending angels did explain
There was no reason for alarm,
No chance of reaping any harm,
While walking in the wilderness
So far from home again.

Singing voices — sweet digress! —
Rang out across the plain
Of waving wheat, sun-gold and warm,
And filled her with their charm,
Removing any waywardness,
Rebelliousness, or stain.

"Life is good — without distress —
When angels guide us in the main."
As simple as a school marm,
She listened to the angelic swarm,
Lost deep within its holiness,
Repeating each refrain.

Melissa, in her tattered dress,
Veered off the dusty lane,
The wicker basket on her arm,
Ripe with goodies from the farm,
And met her mother on the grass,
Who welcomed her back home again.

First published on Spillwords Press on August 22, 2022.

Christ's Sorrow

I was not born for pleasure but for pain;
    For blood and thorns and thirst beneath the sun;
And ev'ry man who doubts I am the One
Has lost the only treasure he could gain.
Blasted with hate, betrayed, and marked like Caine,
My fate was sealed; nor was there place to run.
Standing trial and defended by none,
The case was clear; acquittal was in vain.
You hung me high; you nailed me to the cross;
On either side, the outcasts hung with me.
O enemies mine, I died on that hill
With bitterest gall; but mourn not my loss:
You have helped fulfill my great destiny.
My pain is this: — You do not love me still.

**First published in the *Great Poems of Today Anthology*,
1987.**

Hold on to that Dream

To hold a dream in our hearts is a means of survival —
HOPE which buoys the human spirit
And comforts the troubled soul;
A mighty fortress in which to hide from daily cares;
Or a foothold when we stumble and fall.
You were my dream in difficult years:
A shining arrow pointing the way;
A golden sun rising in my line of vision;
And I held on to that dream
When I should have let go.
But some dreams are beautiful,
Perfect, and chaste;
And no amount of cruel living
Can taint their rainbow hues.

If I could reach the core of that dream,

And yet remain sane,

How much better would life be?

First published on Masticadores USA on January 25, 2023.

My Life is a Desert

My life is a desert. Big and brown and empty.
A chill wind blows sand across my heart,
burying it forever.

Cactus needles pierce my feet and hands,
making the blood flow red.
I place the Crown of Thorns upon my head.

Broken and bent, I ascend the Cross.
Hanging like rotten fruit from a dead tree,
I gaze across the barren landscape and cry,
"My God! My God! Why have You forsaken me?"

First published on Masticadores USA on March 21, 2022.

When the Morning Comes

When the morning comes,
Sun will shine with a different light,
Earth will glow in a brand-new way,
Moon will dance to a gayer tune,
Clouds of pain will float away.
Broken hearts will beat again,
Empty eyes will see new life,
Throats will open up and sing,
Hands will break the chains of strife.
Birds will chirp a loud hello,
Bees will buzz a soft hooray,
Wolves will greet the transformed world
With howls of joy on this new day.
Loving hearts will make new peace,

Working hands will stop and play,

Faces shining at the dawn

Will be transfigured as we pray.

When the morning comes.

First published on Masticadores USA on January 15, 2023.

Legacy

A handful of trinkets.

All that remains of a life which spanned for sixty years
Through childbirth labor and marital pain,
Poverty and hunger and religious faith.
Everything you touched and cherished and dreamed,
Lost forever to mildew and decay,
And the least which survives —
Just a tiny fragment of yesterday.
The old home place no longer stands:
Its groaning walls were bulldozed to the ground;
And the Dutiful Daughter who stayed by your side
Rots away in a back ward dungeon.
How you would writhe and torment in your grave,
Realizing the legacy you left behind
Is nothing more than ashes and dust;
As dead as yourself; and mourned as much.

First published in the *New American Poetry Anthology*, 1988.

Published on Masticadores USA on August 9, 2022.

Boudica's Soliloquy

F oul deeds of war have broken me.
　　Come, smell the blood! Hear the moans of the dying!
The corpses of my daughters lay silently at my feet,
Shamed and murdered by our Roman tormentors.
Colchester and London — what glorious victories! —
The blood flowed freely from Roman wounds.
They howled in rage as they died. How we cheered!
But Rome's crawling legions caught us in their snare,
And now, we are vanquished.
Britannia is no more. Weep for a chastised people!
No longer Queen, I am marked for death.
No longer Mother, I will not be consoled.
No longer Wife, I burn with revenge.

I lift the flask of poison to my lips, tasting the bitterness in my mouth.

I will lie here with my daughters, my shield across my breast

And my spear by my side, and welcome Death with honor.

First published in the *Wounds I Healed: The Poetry of Strong Women Anthology*, 2022.

My Grave

I think that I shall never crave
  A home as lovely as a grave.
A restful place deep in the ground
Without a trace of light or sound.
A grassy mound high on a hill,
Host to yellow daffodil.
And when the snow begins to fall,
I will not be disturbed at all.
A pleasant park is all I need
And visitors who stop to read
The granite marker at my head:
"Rest in Peace to All the Dead!"

First published in the November 2011 issue of *Underneath the Juniper Tree*.

The Age of Elegance

V elvet, lace, satin,
        Silk, brocade;
Long, billowy dresses
With tight bodices
Cut low and alluring.
Fluttering fans
And white hair piled high
As a snow-capped mountain
On heads delicately balanced
On long, slender necks.

Velvet, lace, satin,
Silk, brocade;
Tight breeches

And tailor-made jackets
Elegantly embellished;
Sheer white stockings
Tightly pulled up the legs;
Pilgrim shoes with shiny brass buckles
And scarlet high heels.
Lacy handkerchiefs,
Gold snuff boxes,
And fans conveying
Secret messages to lady-loves,
And mistresses already married.

Velvet, lace, satin,
Silk, brocade;
Drawing-room comedies,
String quartets,
And illicit love-making
In the gold-leaf box seats,
Hidden by gold-leaf grapevines
And golden bunches of grapes.
The Age of Elegance, indeed,
And the Age of Grace.

First published on The Skeptic's Kaddish on July 8, 2022.

The Sleeping Beauty

L ying there in sweet repose,
  Lips as red as any rose,
The Sleeping Beauty rests her head
Upon a gold and velvet bed;
Golden tresses fair displayed
Around the shoulders, softly laid,
Bedecked in sequined, jeweled dress,
Her slender hands across her breast.
Fair Maid! — What evil cast you here
To sleep a full one hundred year
Until a Prince with noble pride
Into the castle court should ride
And climb the steeply winding stair
To find a maid with golden hair

Lying on a couch asleep,

Lost in dreaming long and deep,

And drop upon the tender lips

A kiss so pure the magic slips.

And, lo! — the eyelids flutter wide

And see a vision at her side:

A handsome Prince so near and nigh,

The maiden cannot help but sigh

And stretch out pleading hands to him

Who kissed her softly on a whim,

And thanking him with grateful smile,

Requests of him to stay a while.

The Prince proves better than a guest

And presses her against his breast;

Then carries her, swift as the wind,

Upon his horse across the land

To marble castle rising high

Against the purple morning sky.

And when she curtsies to the King,

The Queen presents her with a ring

And crown of jewels sparkling white —

Gifts of softly glowing light —

That bind her to her Prince's life:

No more a maid! — but now, his wife!

First published on Gobblers & Masticadores on February 4, 2023.

Just Me and the Clock

L ong hours of night creep slowly by.

Tick... Tick... Tick... Tick...

The clock clangs one.

I am utterly alone.

Just me and the clock.

Tock... Tock... Tock... Tock...

My cares all ceased with the setting sun,

But that clock keeps screaming in my ears.

All I crave is peace

And silence:

No ticking time bomb exploding in my head.

I don't care about the passing hours.

Darkness brings a halt to all activity,

Calms my rattled nerves, soothes my racing heart,

Eases the tension of body and soul.

My brain longs to sleep,

Escape the daylight nightmare,

Roam through the corridors and landscapes of dreams

Fashioned from the fabric of my own imagination.

The rich silk of slumber evades me,

And my mind grows weary of the hypnotic beating

Of the hours in my head.

The clock clangs two,

And I'm finally through

With the savage sound in my ear.

I pick up the clock and hurl it at the wall,

Cursing as it bursts into broken pieces

Of wood and metal springs and batteries

Falling to the floor.

It can wait until morning

And the sun's rays glaring through the window.

First published on Masticadores USA on March 21, 2023.

The Rusty Tin Can

For years, the rusty tin can lay in the sand,
Beaten by sun, wind, and rain,
Carried down the desert wash by flash floods.
With time, that rusted-out old can
Became a symbol of
Love and hope,
Life and death,
Stability and change.
Photographers earned prizes.
Artists won acclaim.
Poets got published.
All because of a rusted tin can
Lying in the sand.
One day a hiker picked it up,
Threw it in a garbage bag,
And tossed it in the trash.

First published on Masticadores USA on September 22, 2023.

The Smile

I fell in love
  With the boyish grin
That crinkled your eyes
And made them sparkle
Like diamonds
In two muddy pools.
Blushing,
Your cheeks reddened
As if kissed by the sun.
Your beard caught fire
In the afternoon sunlight,
And my heart fluttered
Like a thousand Valentines
Turned loose in my chest.

First published on Chewers & Masticadores on November 16, 2023.

Psychology

A psychologist by trade,
    She brought order from chaos,
Splicing together the broken threads
Of fragile minds:
Listening for the right tone,
The right inflection, the right notes
To harmonize the deepest
Fears and desires of her clients.
But, in her own disordered brain,
She heard the voices of *her* people,
Day and night,
Crying out from the death camps,
Screaming from the gas chambers,
While men in black jackboots
Goose-stepped through the square,
Claiming victory over her crumbling world.
When the Alzheimer's bore deep into her brain,

Like a hungry insect,
And consumed the last of those dreadful sounds,
She embraced the silence, like a long-lost Lover,
And slept peacefully.

First published on Spillwords Press on June 18, 2022.

The Girl on the Bus

The bus driver watched you in the mirror,
His eyes wide with fear,
When you stood up in the middle of the bus,
Crying like a terrified child.
Passengers waited with bated breath,
Wondering what you would do.
The sharpness of your pain
Pierced me like a sword,
Deep in my belly,
And I reached for you.
My fingers clutched your purple dress
With urgent appeal,
And you looked at me with mournful eyes,
Red-rimmed and afraid.

"Everything will be okay, " I said,

Soothingly, as if anything I could say

Could erase the pain.

Your wailing stopped,

Like a passing storm,

And a flicker of light

Seemed to shine in the deep water-pools of your eyes.

You stumbled down the steps

At the next bus stop,

And I watched you hurry down the street

In perfect calm.

First published on Spillwords Press on November 17, 2022.

The Old Man at the Piano

H is wrinkled fingers
        lovingly touched
the yellowed keys
of the battered upright
and he began to play
a sentimental song from long ago
when Julie danced
and Helen sang
and Lola sat beside him on the bench
pounding a playful duet.
The war was raging then
and at night the sirens blared
calling the people of the city
into underground hiding.

They clung to each other in the dark
while bombs exploded
and buildings collapsed
and smoke filled the war-torn city.
We have to live! We have to survive!
they cried in their hearts
not knowing if their houses
remained intact
not knowing if there was anything left
but memories
scattered pieces
of treasured greeting cards
postcards
and faded photographs.
In the morning
the light would come
shining through the darkness
and the wind would blow
driving away the smoke
and they congratulated one another
on surviving another day.

First published on Literary Revelations Journal on August 15, 2023.

This Land is in My Blood

This land is in my blood
    And my blood is in this land.
I will pick up arms and fight for it.
I will fight for what is mine.
My blood, sweat, and tears
Fertilized this soil.
The crops grow strong and rich
With life-giving nectar.
They nourish my family
And sustain my community.
My country is vast and proud,
Strengthened by the wealth
Of nutrient-rich soil.
The land is in my blood.

The blood is in my land.
And I will die for it.

First published on Gobblers & Masticadores on January 7, 2023.

Springtime

S pringtime struggles to survive
    The clasping arms of winter,
Stirring up the honey-hive
And bringing forth the flower.

She hastens to restore the sun:
The melting snows recede;
And when the sap begins to run,
The worm returns to feed.

A flock of sparrows in the sky;
A big, red-breasted robin
Perched to catch a passing fly,
His little heart a-throbbin'.

Daffodils with yellow heads
Bobbing in a row;

Rich brown fields and grassy beds
Waiting for the plow.

Winter, dying in the wake
Of Springtime's warmer rain,
Thaws the river and the lake
And disappears again.

**First published in the *World Poetry Anthology*, 1987.
Published in the *Best New Poems of 1988* anthology.**

Summer Eden

O, would the gaiety of summer last forever,
  I would lie content in the summer sun,
Lazing away the hours in pleasant dreams,
Drifting, ever drifting, into nothingness;
And I would not weep for lost tomorrows
Or mourn the passing of yesterdays,
For blue skies are forever,
Timeless, changeless, infinite;
And I would not weep for the passing of love,
For love is a flighty thing,
Lofty and intangible,
And difficult to possess;
But give me a whole wide world of bright todays,
And I will be happy!
Give me the sun at my back
And the earth at my feet,
And I will not cry,

For these things are beautiful

And easy to touch.

Let me live my life in the Eden

Of God's creation —

I will be content to die.

First published on Masticadores USA on June 21, 2022.

Sonnet to the Moon

Somehow, I always miss the yellow moon
    That shines somewhere at the end of summer.
I see the stars on their velvet bed, soon
To be lost to the milky-white winter,
But Moon, I only see thee in autumn,
When the air is sweet and pungent with Death.
Then my senses 'waken from their doldrum,
And I long to cling, with icy-white breath,
To thy big, round fulness frozen brightly
In the eastern sky. Then I want to touch
Thy silky-smooth face gazing down nightly;
I want to raise my open hands and clutch
The silvery-white glow falling softly,
Like a satin gown, all around thee.

First published on Masticadores USA on October 3, 2022.

O Thou, England!

A way, away in a distant land
    More green and mild
Than a summer's day;
More grey and wild
Than an ocean bay,
O thou, England! — Verdant isle of my dreams!
Fallen anew
On the ripened arbor,
Sea mist and dew
Shroud the ocean harbor:
My heart yearns to wade through thy soaking sand
And ramble along thy running streams!

So far, so far — and yet, so near
Thy splendid beauty lies,
A sparkling jewel among the blue
Of ocean, sea, and skies!

And would I could, I'd wish it true,

O thou, England! — How kettles then would madly boil!

Blazing fires would crackle and snap,

Scones would bubble and rise;

Glad would I roam thy wooded map

In harmony with the coveted prize:

Down would I bend to drop a tear

And kiss thy wet and fertile soil.

First published on Masticadores USA on November 10, 2022.

April Showers

I looked into the heavens
    And saw the face of God.
He was a kindly gentleman
And not too very loud.
He wore a watch upon his vest
Which gave the time of day.
He looked at it: "The time has come,"
Was all he had to say.
And soon a gentle rainfall
Came from the April sky.
It kissed my wondering up-turned face
And poked me in the eye.
But then a very curious thing
Did happen at my feet.
A tiny flower sprouted up,
All blooming and complete.
It opened up its tiny leaves,

Embracing fast the rain,
And if I ever doubted God —
I never did again.

First published on Gobblers & Masticadores on April 8, 2023.

First Snow

The first white snow of winter
Falls softly on the ground;
The world looks like a fairyland
With snowflakes all around;
The trees dress up like fairies
Dancing on the snow: —
Magic happens everywhere
The fairies dance, you know.

I love the first white winter storm,
The air is cold and frosty;
I stay indoors where it is warm,
But through the windows, I can see
How suddenly the world turns white
And disappears beneath the snow;
The season changes overnight
From autumn's bright to winter's glow.

First published on Gobblers & Masticadores on December 2, 2023.

Coyote

I see you there, hiding in the brush,
  Your tawny colors perfectly blending with nature's camouflage.
How silently you positioned yourself
To watch me dishing up the food that you take for granted.
I hear you say: "Oh, silly human, I've fooled you into thinking
That I need your help to survive — after all, I am called the Trickster
—

When really, you need me to satisfy some hunger inside yourself."
And, that may be true, but I say to you: "Look at yourself, Coyote,
And how healthy you are because of that food. Who's fooling who?
Last summer, you were nothing but skin and bones.
Your fur looked rough and discolored,
Your belly sunken, your ribs barely covered by thin skin.
You know a good thing when you see it, so let's continue to be
friends.
  Please, take my food, and allow me to take spiritual sustenance from
you."

Coyote looked at me with wisdom and understanding and ate the food.

First published on Masticadores USA on September 27, 2022.

Where Shall We Go

Where shall we go since the old home place is gone?
Mama's gone, and Papa's gone;
All the little children have long since grown
And live in the city with children of their own.
Tell me, where shall we go
For birthdays and Christmas and Sunday stew?
Grandma is gone; the recipe she knew
For blueberry pie is lost now, too.
What shall we do?
The old home place is vanished now,
No longer fields will feel the plow
Or hands reach into the apple tree.
Old Brutus is gone. But what about we?
The old home place lives in our hearts,
With memories of quilting arts
And canning beans fresh from the vine
And laundry hanging from the line.

Summer's fun and winter's sleep
Remembered in our hearts so deep,
The pictures glow and come alive —
Fond memories of the family hive
That buzzed and blustered all year round
And gradually fell apart and wound
The ties that bind around the tree
Of family blood and history.

First published on Masticadores USA on December 23, 2022.

Dreamcatcher

I n the end, it was all a dream,
    A fantasy born of longing and need,
A dreamcatcher made of spider silk
And feathers glistening in the moonlight.
You were my nightmare, caught in the web,
Haunting my restless sleep.
How I dreaded meeting you again!
Night after night, running to escape,
Hunting for shelter — someplace safe —
A place to hide, a place to think —
Oh, save me!

In the end, it was all a dream,
And when the hushed hues of dawn
Broke across the sky,
You melted away,
Like a heated piece of wax,

Through the silken web,
And I never saw you again.

First published on Masticadores USA on April 21, 2023.

Separation

Across the void of outer space
      I reach for you
Calling your name
But emptiness answers
Cold and black
Stars stare icily
The old moon glows
And all the wonders of the universe
Should be ours forever
But our spirits soar to opposite ends
And all is hopelessly lost

First published in the *American Poetry Anthology*, 1988.
Published on Masticadores USA on August 25, 2023.

Grief

Darkness descends,
   Like perpetual night,
Obscuring the light
Of your being.
Darkness falls,
Like the curtain of death,
Snuffing out the joy
Of your existence.
I cannot see you.
I cannot touch you.
I cannot reach you
Through the blackened veil.
You fade away into the abyss,
And I cannot hold you.
Oh, light of my life,
Come back to me!
Don't slip into the shadows of nothingness!

Don't leave me where I cannot

Find you —

Far away —

In the murky depths —

Beyond my mortal understanding.

I will never find you again.

First published on Masticadores USA on October 22, 2023.

The Alternative

I watched you mount your chestnut horse with dignity and grace.

    Sitting proudly in the saddle, your boots snug in the stirrups,

You held the reins with your right hand,

The riding crop with your left.

My heart cringed at the sight of that handsome face.

Brown hair curling under a tall hat,

Crisp white lace at your throat,

Your dark eyes shone in the afternoon light,

And you reminded me — again —

That you were off to see your mistress,

Though left unsaid.

My husband — my Lord — my benefactor —

A cruel master indeed.

The Marquis de Sade

Tortured his victims with whips

To achieve gratification.

You torture me with sweet smiles

And encouraging gestures of affection,

Masking the darkness underneath.

Holding me in the vice grip of your command,

My world shrinks smaller and smaller.

You crush me with your capricious punishments and rewards.

You push me to the brink of madness,

Trying to conform to your iron will.

My psyche rebels against you,

My body yearns to run.

Run to the cliffs, the voices call.

I lift my skirts, yielding to their enticement.

The grass parts beneath my flying feet.

Go after her, your voice bellows to the servants.

They take off behind me,

Struggling to catch up.

I hear your horse dance restlessly

In the distance.

Your pride will not allow you to chase after me.

The grassy precipice looms ahead.

I slow down and walk to the edge,

Marveling at the vast green sea below.

The wind blows my hair against my face,

And I feel free!

If the minister is right,

And we transcend to another world,

Then Death seems the better alternative.

I spread my arms wide,

Like the seagulls circling overhead,

And jump.

First published on Masticadores USA on November 29, 2023.

Winter Thorns

I carried a bouquet of winter thorns
    Down the aisle of our wedded bliss.
Sweet summer roses could not survive
The vacillations of tumultuous Love.

Heart to heart and soul to soul,
We united as one,
Experiencing all the joy and sorrow
That Life could afford.

When Death overshadowed us,
Our Love lived on,
Wandering through the ages
Until we found each other once again.

How strange to reunite in other forms!
Different faces, different hands.

But our need for one another never changed.

Our passion consumed us,

Burning us to the core.

Our minds melded into one brain.

Deep currents ran between us.

Spoken words could not convey what we felt.

Silently, we heard each other's thoughts.

Your heart called to mine,

And I responded.

When the Angel of Death

Brought me home to heaven,

I copiously wept,

Begging to go back home to you.

The gates of heaven slammed shut behind me,

And I fell to earth,

Calling your name.

The cycle began all over again.

First published on Masticadores USA on December 26, 2023.

The Look

You sidled up in your Z71
  With the window rolled down,
A slight smile tilting your cruel mouth.
You mean, controlling bastard,
I thought, imagining the worst.
We locked eyes through your sunglasses,
And I knew then
There was no getting out of it
And no going back.
I felt the web spinning around me,
Catching me in its sticky silk.
I'm your prisoner now!
The thought stuck in my head
Because you had never looked at me that way before.
Neither of us spoke a word,
But the message that passed between us was undeniable.
Our fates were sealed.

First published on Chewers & Masticadores on October 22, 2023.

Narcissus

You want me to run to you,
    Like an eager little girl,
Fling myself at your feet,
And declare undying love for you.
You want me to worship
The root of your manhood —
That most ancient of idolatry —
Revering its abundant gift.
You want me to crawl to you
On my hands and knees
With apologies and ardent kisses,
Begging for your approval.
You want me to bow to your genius
And defer to your authority,
Relinquishing my own independence.
You want me to suffer in the darkness
Of your absence

And rejoice in the light of your return,

Renewed by your life-giving force.

You molded me into a reflection

Of your own warped desires,

Dangled me from a string,

Played the puppet master

On the stage you built.

Like the beautiful Narcissus,

You gazed too long into a pool of clear water,

Fell in love with your own brilliance,

And destroyed us both.

First published on Hotel Masticadores on December 14, 2023.

Shattered Glass

S hattered glass
could not
cut deeper
the fine jagged edges
piercing the soul
with precision accuracy

how many times
did you laugh
at the pain
preferring to use it
as balm
for your own
flagging ego

ghost man
invisible

never there
a fleeting memory
in the daylight

how is it possible
to love a ghost

First published on Masticadores USA on April 4, 2022.

On Cupid's Broken Wings

On Cupid's broken wings,
    He landed at my door,
An instrument with broken strings,
No music at his core.
His arm wrapped up in dirty slings,
His leg — an oozing sore,
I welcomed him, and my heart sings
With love, and so much more!

With honeyed lips, I kissed him,
Reflecting on the art
Of healing broken seraphim
With music from the heart:
A golden lyre and a whim

To feel the lover's dart
Deep in my chest, O cherubim! —
Aim true, and never part

From me again, but stay —
And shelter in the womb
Of calming balms and ecstasy,
Such sweetness in this humble home!
Such magic in the healer's play!
From the cradle and the tomb,
A captured heart will run away.
But free me, and I will not stray.

First published on Spillwords Press on February 14, 2023.

Passion

P assion burns, hurts, scars
    The tender flesh of my heart,
Feeling life again.

First published on Spillwords Press on June 17, 2023, with Dawn Pisturino's Author Interview.

Bricks

You fell on me like a ton of bricks,
        Crushing my bones,
Tearing my flesh,
Smashing my heart into a bloody mess.
You set out to destroy me,
Piece by bloody piece,
Using what was left to rebuild
The wall of your own self-worth.
Your prying, spying eyes follow me.
You stretch my tender nerves
To the breaking point,
Leaving them painful and raw.
My stomach churns and ties in knots
From constantly listening for you.
You torched me with the flames of your fury
When I refused to talk to you
By the side of the road.

I was too afraid.

If I feared you then,

Imagine how I fear you now!

But my feelings never matter.

It's all about YOU,

Your cruel tricks designed to diminish me and break me down.

I wake up crying in the middle of the night

In the midst of shadowy dreams about you.

Your face looms over me, and I feel your power.

Control. Possession. Getting your own way at any cost.

That's your *modus operandi*.

And you hate that I keep my distance

Away from you

And resist your domination.

You played a new trick Monday,

Sending your proxy to spy on me.

The car drove slowly past the house

As I sat on the porch reading a book.

I did not recognize the car or the driver,

But he looked at me and grinned.

An hour later he returned,

Repeating the operation.

Were you in the passenger seat?

I could not tell. But somehow,

The man knew where to go and what to do.

Your fingerprints were unmistakable.

I felt angry, humiliated, and belittled.

I am not a dog on a leash

Or a monkey on display at the zoo.

I removed all the extra shrubbery

Along the road to better see you.
I removed all the chairs from the porch
To defy you.
Maybe you will finally get the message and disappear.

First published on Spillwords Press on August 12, 2023.

You and I

P EOPLE
     can only take
so much pain
and trauma
until they shut down
and tune out
and wish it all away.

YOU
never understood
how much pain
you caused
to others.

You died.
And so, we parted,
never really knowing one another.

How sad!

First published on Literary Revelations Journal on August 15, 2023.

Ordinary Things

H e fell in love
Watching her do ordinary things:
The wave of her hand, while saying farewell,
Cut him to the core, making him want to stay;
Rolling pie crust on a floured board,
Back and forth, back and forth,
Until the rhythm lulled him into dreamless sleep;
Kneading the dough for fresh-baked bread,
A sensuous massage in his own mind,
Fold over, fold over, and punch;
The way she smelled the towels right out of the dryer
And carefully folded them for the linen closet.
He loved the way the sunlight streaked her hair
In the middle of the day while cutting roses,
And kissed away the drop of blood that clung
To her slender finger after the thorn left it there.
She smiled at him then, and they both knew:

It's the ordinary things that make love real.

First published on Gobblers & Masticadores on October 1, 2022.

The Squatter

You crawled inside my head,
Took up residence without permission,
Rearranged the furniture in my brain,
And refused to be evicted.

You clawed your way into my heart,
Tore my flesh to bloody shreds,
Played the instruments of my emotions,
And refused to be silent.

You bulldozed the fortress of my resistance,
Broke the walls of my desire,
Found the gems of my dismay
And the keys to my existence.

Slowly dying from the poison of your embrace,
Slowly dwindling from the

Sheer magnetic power of your possession,
I am lost and cannot find myself.

First published on Gobblers & Masticadores on September 2, 2023.

Baudelaire

When i saw you there
    lying on the cold stone slab
your virgin beauty pure as white marble
i remembered why i loved you
and all the promises we made

you no longer see me
except in dreams far away
you no longer hear me
except when celestial angels
open your ear with a golden horn

but i can touch you
and suckle the cold white breast
as empty as your heart
and kiss the waxen lips
devoid of blood

your infinite beauty
is so much more
than your finite body
could ever bear
in this suffering world

someday my soul
will follow you into the ether
and find you smiling
like a gleeful child
in the arms of god

First published on Masticadores India on January 3, 2023.

He Loved His Dogs

His whiny, high-pitched Southern drawl
    Made her skin crawl.
He never seemed to shave,
Reeked of cigarettes and weed,
And flashed his yellow teeth
With childish grins and empty words,
Seeking babyish attention.
He wore his baseball cap backward,
Pulled low on his head,
And cruised the backroads of Alabama
In a clunky white pickup truck,
Looking for God knows what,
And God knows who,
Letting his dogs hang out the window
And yap at the passing world.
But he loved those dogs;
And that's not half bad, right?

When his mama died one lonely night,
He howled at the moon
Like a wounded animal,
And then forgot her.
And when another woman's body
Was recovered from a ditch,
Broken like a China doll,
He hid in the basement,
Clinging to his dogs.
They licked his sweaty face,
Leaned in close for soft caresses
From his rough, calloused hands,
And snarled at the police
Who broke in
And arrested him there.

Even the creeps of this world
Have mothers
And girlfriends
Who try to make them whole.
But he loved his dogs
More than family
And friends —
And that's not half bad, right?

First published on Masticadores India on May 20, 2023.

The Listener

As a small child,
I lay in my small bed,
Listening to the mourning doves
Crying softly, "Coo-hoo! Coo-hoo!"
From the woods across the road
In the early morning light.

At night, the owls called to me —
"Who's there? Who's there?" —
A comforting lullaby that
Quieted my childish fears
And lulled me fast to sleep.

The thunder spoke to me
When the rain called my name,
Throwing his fierce lightning bolts
Across the black, menacing sky.

And when the storm passed away,
A hungry mosquito berated me,
Demanding a bloody feast.

~

The world is not a silent place.
Nor a place of peace.

~

As I grew,
The sounds of life grew louder:
Crashing metal when a truck turned over on the icy road.
My mother screaming,
My father shouting,
Then silence. . . when the unknown driver breathed no more.

First published in *Hidden in Childhood: A Poetry Anthology*, 2023.

I HATE SNAKES

*D*on't go into the swamp!
　　　But we ignored them,
For we were great explorers,
Hunting for lost civilizations
And buried treasure
In the deepest jungles of Africa.
We plowed through the snake grass,
Climbed over rotting tree trunks,
Hung from wild grape vines,
Chattering like monkeys.
And we never considered the dangers
Lurking in our "jungle."
The old summerhouse lay hidden
Among tangled green bushes
And thorn-studded berry brambles,
Overlooking the banks of the St. Joseph River.
I pushed open the creaky door to look inside

And froze in shock at what I saw:

Slithering, crawling, scaly snakes

Formed a moving carpet on the floor,

Entwining in an intimate embrace,

Lying together in a clump of shimmering bodies,

Moving slowly and surely in the rotten shadows.

We beat a hasty retreat

And never visited our "jungle" again.

And that's why, even today,

I HATE SNAKES!

First published in *Hidden in Childhood: A Poetry Anthology*, 2023.

Dirty Donald

Dirty Donald!
His hair, full of lice,
Grows down to his shoulders,
A haven for mice.

His teeth are all rotten,
Mildewed and black,
His tongue is so long,
He could pass for a yak.

His breath stinks of corpses
Dug fresh from their graves,
A delicate morsel
He constantly craves.

He glares at the ravens,
Surrounding his head,

With murderous eyes,
Pronouncing them dead.

Then yanks out their feathers
And nibbles their toes,
Lining them up
In neat little rows.

His clothes are so tattered,
The buzzards all say,
"What a fine-looking fellow!
Let's eat *him* today!"

First published on Underneath the Juniper Tree on July 17, 2011.

Published in the August 2011 issue of *Underneath the Juniper Tree*.

Chelsea had a Little Lamb

Chelsea had a little lamb,
     Its fleece was black as soot.
And everywhere that Chelsea went,
That lamb was underfoot.

It followed her to school until
The cooking class went wild
And served that lamb with mint and dill,
One chop for every child!

First published in the Winter 2011 issue of *Underneath the Juniper Tree*.

The Dentist

N ow I've got you in my chair,
    You're not going anywhere.
So open wide, let me in,
And let the painful games begin!
See that molar on the right?
It's in the socket way too tight.
Here's my plier. Please don't move.
I'll pry that sucker from its groove!
Look, there's a cavity over there.
My drill's all ready. Please don't stare!
My hands are shaking, can't you see?
I need your confidence in me.
Oops! The blood is squirting out.
I didn't mean to make you shout!
Your bloody tongue is in my hand.
Sit down! Don't even try to stand!
Come back! I need to suture in —

Oh well, another toothless grin.

First published in the April 2012 issue of *Underneath the Juniper Tree*.

Down in the Graveyard

D own in the graveyard by the old oak tree
   Roamed an old mother zombie and her little zombies three.
"Fresh meat!" cried the mother. "Tastes sweet!" cried the three.
And they ripped out the intestines from the caretaker, Lee.

Down in the graveyard by the mausoleum door
Lived an old mother werewolf and her little wolfies four.
"Fresh fat!" howled the mother. "Tastes great!" howled the four.
And they tore into the belly of the visitor, Lenore.

Down in the graveyard by the rusty old gate
Hung an old mother vampire and her little vampies eight.
"Fresh blood!" squeaked the mother. "Tastes good!" squeaked the
eight.

And they sank their greedy fangs into the gravedigger, Nate.

First published in the September 2012 issue of *Underneath the Juniper Tree.*

The Screaming Skull

The skull screams when the moon is bright,
Warning of evil a-foot in the night,
Calling to phantoms hidden from sight,
Keeping them all at bay.

Shrieking aloud when the zombies fight,
It glows in the darkness, waking with fright,
Shivering children, crying for light,
Fearful 'til break of day.

High on a shelf, when the bats take flight,
The dead skull cries with all its might,
Disrupting dreams, however slight,
Sending them all away.

First published on Danse Macabre du Jour on October 30, 2013.

The Ghost

Creeping footfalls on the stair warn me that a ghost is there.
Shivering in my bed with fright, the door creaks open. . .
I TOLD YOU HE WAS REAL!
(good night)

First published on Danse Macabre du Jour on October 30, 2013.

The Fairies

D eep within the forest,
          Inside a magic ring,
Fairy lads pluck at their harps
While fairy maidens sing.
Queen Mab, arrayed in starlight,
Sits upon her chair,
Plotting all the dirty tricks
No other folk would dare.
Last spring, they stole poor Margaret,
Sound asleep in bed.
They laid her in the Irish Sea
With stones beneath her head.
The fishes kept close vigil,
Traditional at wakes.
"Too bad," remarked a hungry shark.
"A lovely corpse she makes!"

First published on Danse Macabre du Jour on October 30, 2013.

About the Author

Dawn Pisturino is a retired registered nurse in Arizona whose international publishing credits include poetry, short stories, and articles. A Mystery Writers of America and Arizona Authors Association member, she is working on another book of poetry, a collection of published short stories, several novels, and a memoir.

Author website: www.dawnpisturino.org

Author blog: www.dawnpisturino.wordpress.com

www.ingramcontent.com/pod-product-compliance
Lightning Source LLC
Chambersburg PA
CBHW060542130626
46553CB00002B/869